Typhoon Etiquette
Katrina Naomi

VERVE
POETRY PRESS
BIRMINGHAM

PUBLISHED BY VERVE POETRY PRESS
Birmingham, West Midlands, UK
https://vervepoetrypress.com
mail@vervepoetrypress.com

All rights reserved
© 2019 Katrina Naomi

The right of Katrina Naomi to be identified as author of this work has been asserted in accordance with section 77 of the Copyright, Designs and Patents Act 1988.

No part of this work may be reproduced, stored or transmitted in any form or by any means, graphic, electronic, recorded or mechanical, without the prior written permission of the publisher.

FIRST PUBLISHED APR 2019

Printed in Birmingham by Positive Print

ISBN: 978-1-912565-20-7

CONTENTS

Today I Saw Mount Fuji	6
Self-Introduction	7
I Believe in Gender Equality	8
On Trying to Write in Matsumisho, a Place Bashō Found Impossible to Write About Because of its Beauty	9
Greetings from Yamanashi	10
In a Plum Grove	12
Typhoon Etiquette	13
Tanka for Hiroshi	15
Versions of Yasuaki Inoue's Haiku	16
In the Room Specifically for Resting at the Tokyo National Museum	18
First Tea Ceremony	19
And Today There's a Risk of Bears on the Path	20
Five O'Clock Tanka	21
Versions of Dakotsu Iida's Haiku	22
Interpretation	23
Whoever Said the British Invented the Queue Had Never Been to Japan	24
Where Only the Gods May Walk	26
Michiyo Plays the Koto	27
What Arrival Feels Like	28

Notes

for Michiyo Takano and Maura Dooley

Typhoon Etiquette

*A poem is the cross-section of a whirlwind,
do not nail it too soon to the page, and then only
in such a manner as it will soon fly off the page.*

– Peter Redgrove, 1970 notebook no. 39, SUA archive

Today I Saw Mount Fuji

through a glass wall
at the new university
I nearly fell down the clean staircase

It was like seeing the *Mona Lisa* for the first time
only better
I felt I might cry

or drop my books
or have a stupid expression
and, for once, I honestly didn't care

Self-Introduction

Variations on a theme after Shuntarō Tanikawa

I'm a tall middle-aged woman
with a quiff
For over half a century
I've been bossed about
by men and their words

I like mountains, I like moors
I love swimming in the sea
I'm not so interested in science
and I feel antipathy towards mathematics

I am long-sighted
and resent wearing glasses to read
I have no Christian or other altar in my home
but I do have many paintings
that tempt me into my room
I regard sleeping as a necessary duty
Last night I dreamt my partner was murdered

What I'm writing here is factual
and yet I feel a reluctance to put things into words
I have a sister and no children
no pets of any sort

I spend most of the summer in shorts
The words I write are replacing those
of the men who bullied me

I Believe in Gender Equality

I too can be destructive
wanting fame at any price

my legs sticking out of the sea
in a fabled painting

but this has been done before
I'm too late for Auden

Let me find out about *hari-kiri*
I'm not one for feathers and glue

I've a boarding pass
in my own name

I've thought of nothing else for months

On Trying to Write in Matsumisho, a Place Bashō Found Impossible to Write About Because of its Beauty

Four hundred years on
I can't help thinking of tsunamis
and whether my hotel room is high enough

and what would happen to those 275 islands
in the bay where the water this morning
is a pale jade, flat-flat, perfectly swimmable

Bashō wouldn't have had the 6 am call
to work over a loudspeaker
I almost didn't recognise its kind of gaiety

I'd like to have written about this place
before the arrival of hotels in the cedars
the romantic in me ignoring that even Bashō

needed somewhere to dream of what he wouldn't write

Greetings from Yamanashi

umbrella held high
a woman walks by a stream
red-capped kingfisher

*

naked as winter
we are pale bodies steaming
in what was once rain

*

a lithe fish's blood
is easily washed away
from sushi chefs' hands

*

we lurch in first gear
once in a lifetime visit
but people live here

*

stepping from bright sun
into Kuon-ji temple
a single monk drums

*

clouds hide Mount Fuji
as do grey Venetian blinds
mountains can be shy

*

low-fringed Sayaka
student in my uni class
says she likes to sleep

*

hooded Mount Fuji
almost something sexual
as white clouds retract

*

autumn separates
I've been away from you through
typhoon days and nights

In a Plum Grove

The plums are from all over Japan
I won't eat them
but admire their shapely leaves
which are clinging on
in this typhoon
I also admire a stream surging through
Kenrokuen Garden
emboldened

Umbrellas hurry past
the typhoon hasn't truly hit yet
this is only a taste
By tomorrow there'll be more
umbrellas on the ground
than plums

Typhoon Etiquette

Everything is wet
E v e r y t h i n g
Things are done properly here
For two days you will all struggle with umbrellas
On the third day   the see-through plastic and spoke carcasses
line the kerbs
I wait
for my name and number to be proclaimed across the land
before making my arrival
I don't rush
up the country
that would be inconsiderate
I take each island in turn
a typhoon etiquette
Yaeyama   Miyako   Okinawa   Amami   Tokara   Yakushima
I savour Okinawa   raking
each field   forcing every cane of sugar   every husk of rice
to drink itself daft
You will know of my arrival
via text
in the middle of the night
There's the gathering of winds
the heavy slant
of rain   It is almost a relief for you
The waiting is over
I am here
Some of you bet on my wind speeds
I can perform at a mean 150 km an hour

Most aren't fooled by the lull
after my initial hit
but I love to see those blond tourists
venture from their Best Westerns
flat cameras like amulets
They won't stay for long
I like the streets
empty night or day   when even the crows are silent
then I concentrate
Destruction used to be easier
I'd been taught to savour the *umashi*
of Shibuya's concrete   how it used to crumble
I spun around laughing when they built taller
But they're cleverer than before
With this all-seeing eye
I do my best work   and my worst
Don't be fooled
treesriverscarsseafronts are easy
My life is brief   a few days at most
Respect me
write down my name   worship me in this way
then shake the rope that leads to your gods
see if they are listening

Tanka for Hiroshi

In the jazz bar's warmth
a question falls: Why don't you
know your own poems?

I've no answer; I swirl ice
in a Kirin single malt

Versions of Yasuaki Inoue's Haiku

Pyres of leaves burning
once again in my garden
blazing in the sun

*

In the abundance
of autumn   a baby cries
like a giant fire

*

Blue-eyed billy goat
tilting his horns   suspicious
of the winter sky

*

Today it is cold
like a dead person's make-up
the cold is pure white

*

Step by frozen step
winter comes creeping towards
the naked rock's skin

In the Room Specifically for Resting at the Tokyo National Museum

I have learnt there are many words for kimono,
that none of these garments come out
in my photos, that I'm not interested
in swords, that I like the Edo period
screens, that Japanese art wasn't considered

to be art by the West for centuries,
that the Chinese and Korean influence
waned over 800 years ago, that poetry is written
with a brush or biro, that the script
drops from top to bottom like a waterfall,

that cherry blossom, maple leaves,
chrysanthemums, cranes and lions
are popular motifs, that I don't understand
the attraction of netsuke, that no two tea bowls
are alike, and that I'm really tired, but

I'd settle for a kimono or *furisode*, a *hitoe*,
a *katabira*, a *kazuki*, a *koshimake*, a *kosode*
or even an *uchikake* of the samurai class;
first, I'm going to close my eyes
see what happens when I wake up

First Tea Ceremony

I was thirsty   glad to get out of the rain
A woman in a stern kimono brought us tea
I'd expected a pot   cups with handles
I wish I could remember the bowl's colour,
something of its glaze but I was thirsty
The tea was dark green and frothed
like seaweed soup   We were served so little
I went to ask for more   I was thirsty

I hadn't turned the bowl twice before drinking
hadn't reached out for it with both hands
hadn't drunk with three practised gulps   hadn't
contemplated the bowl after drinking   I remember
enjoying the cake   I wish I'd looked into the bowl
appreciated the empty as well as the full

And Today There's a Risk of Bears on the Path

We have one bear bell between us
fixed to the back of our leader's rucksack
we are to stay close, to chat loudly
but stay close
               and if we surprise a bear
and the bear comes running
our leader says our best defence
is to hold our own rucksack
in front of our body and hope
                            the bear mauls this
instead of our face and torso
and at some point during this procedure
to jab at the bear's eye with a finger –

        that should see it off

Five O'Clock Tanka

Sumo on TV
elsewhere a murmuration
grappling with dusk

each bird dropping like a grain
of salt tossed on the *dohyō*

Versions of Dakotsu Iida's Haiku

Dewdrops on taro
potato leaves reflect a
solemn mountain range

*

An iron windchime
abandoned in late summer
sounds here in autumn

*

I plucked pampas grass
from the stream   feel autumn's weight
shiver on my palm

Interpretation

With thanks to Yamanashi Prefectural Library

I've almost stopped interpreting
yen – all those noughts.
I thought, at first, those notes haven't helped me
write a poem. I recalled a man on Waterloo Bridge
who wrote poems for cash. I offered £2,
received a poem about love on orange paper,
a purple envelope. I could have paid £20, £20,000.
What could a poem be worth and to whom?
How many noughts should I add,
for a favourite poem? And how could it be owned,
no matter how many yen or pounds
in a shiny gold purse? None of these
philosophers in their remarkable robes
can buy such words. A poem's worth
everything and nothing. Perhaps
some of my philosophers understand. And yes,
it has cost me to sit in silence
in this spacious, air-conditioned place,
the philosophers asleep in the close confines
of their dreams. What would Austen say
on the matter? And if I threw these notes,
these dreaming philosophers, from the top
of this building, with its roofline trees,
typhoonish-blue sky, who's to say –
from such a distance – what is money,
who is royalty, what are mere jottings,
and which is a love poem written to a stranger?

Whoever Said the British Invented the Queue Had Never Been to Japan

Here you do not push onto the train from the side
You stand well back and let others off
who, in a moment of exuberance, are released from the sliding doors
like salmon leaping up an escalator
You do not step forward of the red or purple or blue or yellow tape –
demarcating the platform's queues for every type of train –
until the carriage is empty
You might be expected to allow the train an inhalation
of country air after the heat and cloy of Tokyo
You step on, in turn, in this system of deference
The queue being careful to double back
so as not to hinder the formation of other queues for other trains
on a thin platform
or to obstruct passengers with bags or babies or both
This is a polite society

I have benefited from such politeness
such readiness to help a foreigner
Yet one day when the coach arrived
to take a group of poets to the mountains
and the driver, in peaked cap and white gloves
had bowed
given the necessary greetings
when it was time to get on board
no one stepped forward
A flummery of *After you*
No, after you

a ranking of seniority, the more experienced, the better poet
I almost lost it
almost shouted
Can someone just get on the effing bus
But I did what everyone else did
and stared at the recently swept tarmac

Where Only the Gods May Walk

I make the mistake of walking under the Shintō gate
at the shrine to *onsen*
yet another false step
after treading on the restaurant floor in shoes
using the wrong sauce for dipping
refusing another dish when invited
and later
while floating
showing the balls of my feet in the *onsen*
I knew nothing
was nothing
had almost disappeared
in the steam
of my ego

Michiyo Plays the Koto

I'm not sure how much longer I can listen
because this is my last night and this is
goodbye
        I feel a foreigner all over again
as if I've not already spent five weeks here
How little I know
                If nothing else
I recognise melancholy
speaking both of our languages
along the *koto's* wooden body
littered with tiny white Tokyo Towers
This is goodbye to my friend
in grey kimono and mustard *obi*
bent over this almost-zither
                So different
from what I thought I knew

What Arrival Feels Like

Tugging the cold window down
I check myself   worried
I'll feel shy or regretful in some way   unsure
if the tears are caused by the rush of night
air   the thought of you   or the lights of Penzance
their gaudy echo in the bay   or just my eyes' blur
after no sleep for 36 hours   The time has gone
backwards and forwards   I saw two sunsets
on an 11-hour flight   Can that be possible?
I focus   as best I can   on the moon   the stars
the end of the land   knowing I can travel
no further
                I make believe I can see you
way along the platform   After all these weeks
I can   It's you in your green coat from Berlin
I see your black jeans and zebra-print shoes
a bunch of anemones in your left hand   your right
reaches mine as I lean from the train
You hug me as I spill from the journey
Our mouths touch   we say nothing out loud
Now   I step back   look at you
properly   my tears wet
on your cheek
                Our talk on the brief walk home
is of aeroplane food   the shop that's shut down
a politeness that comes of distance
knowing we'll talk and talk over the next few hours
days and months and before morning   we'll be naked

then time and the longing will stop
not just in this act but the moving towards
each other   in understanding each other's lives
again   And I will learn to give up
the sadness   the joy and the normality
of having been alone –
and not be reluctant

NOTES

A general note on names – I have used the Western order of names, ie first name, second name. In Japan, the order is usually reversed.

*

Self-Introduction - Shuntarō Tanikawa was born in Tokyo in 1931 and has published over 60 poetry collections to date.

Typhoon Etiquette – *umashi* refers to something being delicious.

Versions of Yasuaki Inoue's Haiku – Yasuaki Inoue is editor and president of the haiku society *Kakko* (Cuckoo). He has published two collections, *Shiho* and *Kyogoku*. He was born in Nirasaki City, Yamanashi, in 1952. I am grateful to Professor Michiyo Takano of Yamanashi Prefectural University for providing literal translations of Yasuaki Inoue's and Dakotsu Iida's poetry.

Five O'Clock Tanka – *doyhō* is the ring in which sumo wrestlers perform.

Versions of Dakotsu Iida's Haiku – Dakotsu Iida, (1885-1962), also known as 'Dakotsu', published five collections of poetry. He was editor of Unmo haiku journal until his death. He lived in Fuefuki City, Yamanashi.

Interpretation – Yukichi Fukuzawa, (1835-1901), a philosopher, writer and cultural critic is one of the founders of modern Japan. His likeness appears on the 10,000 yen banknote.

Where Only the Gods May Walk – *onsen* is a hot spring bath.

Michiyo Plays the Koto – a *koto* is a large, stringed instrument. An *obi* is a wide belt worn over a kimono.

ACKNOWLEDGEMENTS

My thanks to the editors of *Finished Creatures, Kyoto Journal, Modern Poetry in Translation* and *Poetry Ireland Review* where some of these poems first appeared.
Thank you to all friends in Kofu, including everyone at Yamanashi Prefectural University, particularly Michiyo Takano and her students, and to Yukari Ito and Yasuaki Inoue, to the table tennis group and the Fluunt vegan restauranteurs, and to Miki Matsuura and Hiroshi Kato. My thanks to Andrew Houwen in Tokyo, and to Hiroshi Taniuchi and all the poets of JUNPA in Kyoto.
A big thank you to everyone who has commented on these poems, particularly Penelope Shuttle, Judy Brown and Sarah Barnsley, and to members of Falmouth Poetry Group. Thanks to Maura Dooley and Sally Crabtree for contacts in Japan, to Amy Wack and Gemma Seltzer for encouragement. And to Tim Ridley, as always.
Thank you to my excellent editor, Stuart Bartholomew, and to all of the team at Verve Poetry Press.
Finally, thanks to Arts Council England for an Artists' International Development Award, which enabled me to travel to Japan.

ABOUT THE AUTHOR:

In 2018 Katrina Naomi received a BBC commission for National Poetry Day and recently received an Authors' Foundation Award from the Society of Authors for work on her forthcoming third full collection. Her poetry has appeared in *The TLS, Poetry London, The Poetry Review* and *The Forward Book of Poetry 2017*, as well as on BBC TV's *Spotlight* and Radio 4's *Front Row* and *Poetry Please*. Her latest collection, *The Way the Crocodile Taught Me* (Seren, 2016), was chosen by Foyles' Bookshop as one of its #FoylesFive for poetry.
Katrina was the first writer-in-residence at the Brontë Parsonage Museum in W Yorks. She has a PhD in creative writing (Goldsmiths) and tutors for Arvon, Ty Newydd and the Poetry Society.
www.katrinanaomi.co.uk

BY THE SAME AUTHOR:

The Way the Crocodile Taught Me (Seren, 2016)
Hooligans (Rack Press, 2015)
Charlotte Brontë's Corset (Brontë Society, 2010)
The Girl with the Cactus Handshake (Templar Poetry, 2009)
Lunch at the Elephant & Castle (Templar Poetry, 2008)

https://vervepoetrypress.com
@VervePoetryPres
mail@vervepoetrypress.com